"*The Million-Dollar Sticky Not*
fable that is impossible to pu
is a unique and masterful storyteller in the tradition
of O. Henry and Frank Capra."

~ **Matt Solari,** Creative Director, BRC Imagination Arts

"*The Million-Dollar Sticky Note* is heartfelt, hilarious, and shockingly deep. A tiny tome full of great wisdom dipped in profundity and wrapped in wry humor. With dialogue worthy of Preston Sturges and a concept as cracked as anything Kurt Vonnegut ever dreamed up, it touched me, surprised me, and even gave me a little hope."

~ **Haris Orkin,** award-winning author of *You Only Live Once*

"A wonderful story, told in a lively and compelling way, that carries a powerful and unforgettable message."

~ **Steve Chandler,** author of *Crazy Good*

"R. Lee Procter's *The Million-Dollar Sticky Note* scores a bull's-eye to the heart. Funny, poignant, rewarding and a breeze to read, it contains a profound reminder of a universal truth, a message we really need to hear right now, because it tells us what deep down we already know, that what's important in life is readily available within us all. I encourage every reader to allow this book to work its soulful wonders."

~ **Gil Reavill,** author of *This Land Is No Stranger*

The
Million-Dollar
Sticky Note

The
Million-Dollar
Sticky Note

3 Words that Can Change Your Life

R. LEE PROCTER

MAURICE BASSETT

The Million-Dollar Sticky Note: 3 Words that Can Change Your Life

Maurice Bassett
P.O. Box 839
Anna Maria, FL 34216

Contact the publisher:
MauriceBassett@gmail.com

Contact the author:
milliondollarstickynote@gmail.com

Editing and interior layout: Chris Nelson
Cover design: David Michael Moore

ISBN: 978-1-60025-185-6

Library of Congress Control Number: 2021949451

First Edition

To every great teacher who has shown me the way, including David K. Reynolds, James Hollis and Steve Chandler. And to everyone living on the knife-edge of despair: if I can find peace, so can you.

Contents

The
Million-Dollar
Sticky Note

CHAPTER 1

December 20

I am sitting on a barstool in a neighborhood gin mill admiring the world's most perfect drink: the Irish coffee. I've had a few thousand of these and enjoyed every single one. What's not to like? Coffee to perk you up, brown sugar to speed you up, Irish whiskey to mellow you out, and fatty whipped cream to make it all go down nice and slow. Alcohol, sugar, caffeine, and fat. The Oblivion Cocktail, perfected. I lean forward and slurp a mouthful from the footed mug.

Delicious!

This is the beginning of the end. From here I'll return to my hotel room. I have my baggie of turbo-charged Chinese pharmaceuticals, and I have my note, including instructions on what to do with the body (cremate, and blow the ashes in the face of Patrick Houghton, the rat bastard who fired me from my own company).

I've already enjoyed two Long Island Iced Teas: vodka, tequila, gin, rum, Triple Sec, and a lemon wedge. The wedge is full of life-giving vitamin C and hesperidin, an antioxidant that prevents atherosclerosis. Or it would if I didn't throw away the wedge every time. The two LIITs deliver the delicious nudge into weightless oblivion. Now I need a bump of caffeine to complete my adventure here on earth.

I'm about to chug my Hibernian speedball when . . . hmmm. What's this? Something scrawled on the damp cocktail napkin underneath it:

"Don't do it! What if you're wrong? Take a deep breath and call this number."

I freeze, then blink and stare at it again. What the hell? The whole reason I picked Muggsy's Pub is because of its reputation as the anti-*Cheers*: NOBODY knows my name, or cares. I turn to the bartender, a diffident gent in a black vest who is chatting up a brunette in a sassy, strapless little black dress. He served my drink, so I stare at him for a long moment. He finally turns and cocks a "Refill?" nod at me. I give him a single shake of my head and he turns back to the woman. I survey the rest of the establishment. Five solitary barflies and a glum waitress stare at an NBA game on the big screen TV, sound off. Not even live: a Bulls-Pistons classic from the late eighties. Michael Jordan was an astonishment: someone who, through skill and willpower, could bend reality to help him achieve his destiny.

He is everything I'm not.

"Don't do it!" Somebody hand-wrote this for me personally — somebody who, it seems, knows what I'm about to do. This is beyond weird, since I've only just decided myself. Had to be the bartender . . . but I've never laid eyes on him before tonight, and all he did was put the napkin down. Somebody else could have slipped it onto the top of the stack. Do all the other napkins say this? I lean over the bar. Nope, just the cartoon-pink elephant holding a martini glass in its trunk.

I look at the bartender again. Can't even get him to glance my way this time.

I feel an anxious geyser of bile well up in my chest. I slug back the Irish coffee in two gulps, hoping the wakey sauce will steady me and fix my commitment:

Okay, you can do this. You have both the means and motivation to end your life. You've done enough thinking. You are going to murder yourself, and you will achieve this with a ferocious resolve. You will not screw this up, like you've screwed up everything else in your life, including your marriage, your daughter, and your career. You are steadfast. Resolute. Determined. There is no point in picking up this stupid napkin, folding it once and putting into the inner breast pocket of your sport coat.

Which is what I do. Damn. Am I going to screw this up too? No! Or maybe. Oh probably.

Why spoil a perfect record at the very end?

CHAPTER

2

I've chosen a modest room in my favorite luxury hotel because of the scent: the smell of my childhood. The hotel was brand new when my parents brought me to New York to see *The Music Man*. Lilac, lily zest, ginger and a vanilla finish, like cookies in the oven. That's what I want in my nostrils as I plummet into the infinite wormhole of the Big Sleep.

I think of that bar napkin in my pocket and snort a mirthless chuckle.

What part of hopeless don't you understand? How many times have you pulled out your legal pad, written

"Reasons to Go On Living," and then stared at the blank page while you drank half a bottle of Old Grand-Dad? I've already had second thoughts, and third thoughts . . . I must be on thirty-second thoughts by now. Enough.

I look at the bed. There's my Ziploc sandwich baggie with a double-death portion of heavy-duty, state-certified, executioner-approved powdered Nembutal. This is courtesy of Nick, the Asperger's genius I.T. guy at the ad agency who found it on the "dark web" in China, along with a testing kit and instruction booklet.

The only thing that can stop me now is a spectral intervention, as in *A Christmas Carol*: a heavenly wraith who can illuminate the cosmic gift hidden in my divorce, getting fired from a thriving company bearing my name, and my cancer diagnosis. I've been waiting for this ghost my entire life, only now it's too damn late. Sorry, Mr. Dickens. God bless us every one, except for a certain yours truly.

I take $300 worth of Pappy Van Winkle's Family Reserve twenty-three-year-old, 95.6 proof Kentucky Straight Bourbon Whiskey — that is, one bottle—out of my backpack. The sublime final note of my swan song. I unscrew the top and pour four fingers into a water tumbler. I pick up the baggie of Nembutal. Once I dump it into the Pappy Van Winkle, I'm committed. I will have created an $800 Endless Nightcap. No turning back.

I open the baggie and sniff the drug. No scent. A random memory drifts up: a radio documentary on failed suicides. One guy jumped from the Golden Gate Bridge and survived. He was driven to kill himself by a thrumming voice in his head that kept repeating, "No hope, no hope, no hope." The second he jumped, that voice said, "Ya know, we really could have worked this out . . ."

Hmmm. I try one last time to think of a reason to live, just one reason.

And one comes to me. I take out the bar napkin and read again:

"Don't do it! What if you're wrong? Take a deep breath and call this number."

What if I'm wrong? Impossible. But what if I am? I've spent my life being wrong about everything. I put down the baggie and carry the Pappy Van Winkle over to the bed. I take a generous sip, swish it around my mouth, then savor that rapturous burn down my gullet. Damn, I'll miss that. I pull out my smartphone and dial the number that's scrawled on the napkin. Two rings, then the line's picked up and a woman's voice says,

"Mister Dolan?"

Huh? My name should have been blocked. "Umm, speaking."

"Thanks for calling. We're very sorry to hear about the cancer diagnosis. At least it's not the aggressive kind."

"How the hell do you know that?"

"Oh, we know all about you. It's part of the Service."

"Service?"

"For people who have decided to commit suicide. Tonight, right?

What the . . .? "Ummmmm . . ."

"Chinese Nembutal?"

"R-right." *How could they possibly know this shit? And who were "they"?*

"Well, before you do anything, we'd like to make you an offer."

"Offer? What kind of . . ."

"We'd like to make it in person. Can you meet me tomorrow? Oh let's see, how's about that coffee place in SoHo, the HuggaMug? 11:00 a.m.? You can walk from your hotel."

My head is spinning, and not just from the bourbon. "Look, it's way too late. I've pretty much decided . . ."

"You'll be dead a long time. We're just asking for one day."

"I can't think of a single thing you could tell me . . ."

"What if you're wrong? About everything?"

"What's everything?"

"Who you are, why you're here, what's left to do . . ."

"And you can give me all that?"

"It's what we do."

"I don't . . ."

"C'mon. Worst case, you'll waste one morning with a really good cup of coffee. You can be dead by noon."

"Why can't you tell me on the phone?"

"That's not how the Service works. It has to be a face-to-face meeting." A long pause, then, "What have you got to lose?"

I look at Pappy, then at the death powder. "Okay. But let's make it first thing."

"You name the time."

"Seven, I'm an early riser."

"Good. I'll see you then." She hangs up. Okay, I can make it through one more night with a Pappy Van Winkle sedative.

CHAPTER

3

December 21

She shows up at three minutes to seven and grabs the coffee she's ordered on the way over. I'd arrived at a quarter till so I could doctor up my medium-dark roast with an airline bottle of Bushmills Black Bush (spicy!). She's a pert, stylish African American woman in her late fifties with a helmet of silver-gray hair that sets off her white blouse, black blazer and black pants. She's carrying a large leather handbag that she sets down to shake my hand. "Mr. Dolan, it's a pleasure to meet you. I'm Joan Blair."

I shake her hand. "Delighted. So how do you know so much about me?"

"Have we been wrong about anything so far?"

"Well, no, but . . ."

"Then tell me why it matters." This stops me. Of course it matters!

"Because . . . ummmm . . ." I mumble, then fall quiet.

She fills in the silence. "What matters is that I can help you save your life."

"Uh huh." I like the way she puts that. She isn't here to save my life, just to help me save my own life. Impossible. But still . . . "How?"

She fixes me with a salesman's "closer" gaze. "What if I can give—no, that's not accurate—SELL you a reason to live that you haven't been able to find by yourself? What if I can—and I mean this literally—change your mind?"

I burst out laughing, which morphs into a rasping smoker's wheeze. "So I'm buying something here? Well I've made my living selling things to people, and lady, I'm the hardest of hard sells. What are you selling? Some 'Jesus Loves Me' religious dogma? Dumbed-down Buddhism? A bullshit, happy-thought self-help seminar? A discount lobotomy? Are you going to give me a new identity, move me to Hawaii and help me find my bliss renting boogie boards?"

Still with the gaze. "I'm going to sell you a sticky note."

I cock my head at her. She doesn't change expression, just keeps those smiling, laser eyes focused on me. She's good, I'll give her that.

"A sticky note."

"Right."

"A sticky note that will change my mind, vanish my self-loathing, re-frame my anguish and give me a way to live happily in this fallen world?"

"Right."

"For the first time ever."

"Exactly."

"And how much is this sticky note?" I take a sip of coffee.

"One million dollars." I spray my coffee on her spotless white blouse and gag so hard I get the hiccups. She doesn't stop smiling as she dabs a napkin on her blouse.

"Sorry. So, what exactly is on this million-dollar sticky note?"

"The secret."

"To what?"

"Everything."

"Do you think I'm crazy?"

The gaze continues but the smile vanishes, replaced by concern. "You're the one about to kill yourself, Joe. Being alive is a miracle. It's an astonishing gift, a once-only-in-all-eternity invitation to the cosmic dance. Sure it's also a terror and a heartbreak, but that's part of the dance. That's what makes us real human beings. And you're about to throw it away as if it's nothing. It's not nothing. It's everything. We can help you see that."

"With a sticky note," I say. I don't laugh this time, just break out in a big grin. "Well, sister, I want to hand it to you. This is the toothpick in the shit sandwich of my life, the mother of all idiotic rip-offs." She nods at me, as if she's heard this before. "How many of these million-dollar sticky notes have you sold?"

"Oh, they don't all sell for a million dollars. Some sell for a hundred dollars, some sell for ten million dollars. So far the most expensive sticky note was a hundred and fourteen million dollars. Depends on how much the client has."

"And you think I'm good for a million."

"If you sell your BMW and cash out your Apple stock, you'll just barely make it."

"And then I'll be broke."

"Yes. And it won't make a bit of difference, because you'll be happy."

I wonder if there's something she DOESN'T know about me. "So let's say I have the mother of all brain farts and I write you a check for a million dollars for this sticky note. Let's say I see the three words, and in a blink I know I'm suddenly both suicidal and destitute. I assume my only option is, what, an anguished scream? Gnashing of teeth? Some vivid profanity?"

"Oh no. If you're not completely satisfied, we'll give you a full refund."

My eyes bulge as my face goes slack. What?!? "I'm sorry, did you say . . . a full refund?"

"Of course."

"I hand you the note and get my million back."

"That's right. That's the deal." For the very first time in this exchange I'm actually kind of interested. This is one hell of a sales pitch. Then she adds, "There's just one condition."

"KNEW IT!" I shout. Twelve heads swivel and glare at me. "What's the catch?"

"You don't get your money back right away."

"Oh, I see. Right. So in ten years . . ."

"Three days. Seventy-two hours."

"And after that I can get every single dollar of my money back?"

"Yes. That said, we've never had a case of buyer's remorse. One-hundred percent customer satisfaction. So do we have a deal?"

"So how does this work? Do you get a commission on the sale? What, fifty percent? Half a million?"

"Oh, no. I don't make a thing. It all gets

reinvested."

"In the stock market?"

"In the Service. In helping people like you. And me. I was a customer before I moved into sales. I know what you're going through, because I was where you are now. Only for me it was going to be carbon monoxide in my garage rather than Nembutal."

I can feel my heart thudding in my chest. I'm having a genuine moment. I kinda sorta want to take her up on her offer. But, I mean, come on! A sticky note? With three words? For a million dollars? And after I hand over the million, how do I know she won't be laughing it up with her Russian Mafia cohorts as they jet-ski in Barbados, leaving the world's biggest sucker high, dry, broke and dead?

"Well?" She reaches into her handbag, pulls out an executive folio and takes out a one-page contract on linen cardstock. She offers it to me with a fat Montblanc fountain pen.

"I, ummm . . . Well, look, can I have some time to think it over?"

"You mean, go back to your hotel room, Google around, see if you can discover what kind of scam this is?"

"Exactly."

"Sure. This offer is on the table for forty-eight hours. In two day's time, I'll be back at this coffee shop with the contract and the sticky note. You don't need to bring the money. We trust you."

CHAPTER

4

I open my browser, bring up Google and type in every possible version of "sticky note scam suicide three words." Nothing, just the usual argle-bargle. If this is real, it's quite an operation. No leaks, no rumors, no nothing. Either they exist on some higher plane, or I'm the first (and possibly only) sucker they've ever worked this on. That seems unlikely.

My next move is to Google "happiness three words." Most of the answers are embedded in treacly bromides with words like love, gratitude, and hug. The more interesting answers are singular click bait lists designed to generate web traffic. These include:

- Cigars, hookers, Scotch (lots of Viagra pop-up ads here)

- Pizza, beer, Cubs (male sports blogger)

- Cats, friends, coffee (female: pink website, animated cats, vegan pastry recipes)

Well that was a bust. Okay, I'm going to make one more list. This is personal. These people want my money. Is there some way I can make myself happy spending that million on myself? What would that look like? Let's see . . .

1. Private jet to Las Vegas. Penthouse suite at a premium hotel. Gamble all day, party all night. Heart-stopping bets in private rooms surrounded by rentable female companions.

2. Manhattan. Shows, champagne, limo rides. Live in the penthouse of the Four Seasons till the money runs out, then a swan dive off the balcony.

3. A Million-Dollar World Tour, beginning and ending in Kauai. Collect cocktail

umbrellas from chic bars on seven continents.

Problem is I did some version of all of these when I was riding high in the agency world. I'd always end up poorer, hungover and filled with searing regret. No matter what I did, I was a captive of a looping cranial voice tape saying, "You're supposed to be having fun. You're spending a fortune to have fun! You're not having fun! What's wrong with you??"

I call Joan back and ask for a breakfast meeting the next morning. That still leaves me twenty-four hours before I have to make a decision.

CHAPTER
5

December 22

I consider myself an expert negotiator: one of the best. I know what I want and what I'll pay for it. I'm willing to walk away. I explain to Joan that I'm curious about what's on the note, but it's just not worth a million dollars. I'll happily pay her — or them — twenty thousand dollars for it and forgo the three-day refund offer.

She shakes her head. "The price of the note is a million dollars. There's no point in offering me a hundred thousand, two hundred thousand, or five hundred thousand dollars. A million dollars, in a lump sum payable on delivery."

"You're acting like you don't want to make this deal."

"Oh, I do. I'm sure you can tell what kind of investment we've made in you. Have you noticed that we're the only ones who care whether you live or die?"

"Then why not just give me the note?"

"Because if you pay nothing, you'll think it's worth nothing. We won't have achieved our goal of helping you save your life. This is the big casino, Joe. One hand, cards up. You have to push all your chips to the middle of the table. Only then will the words have the power to help you save yourself."

"Well, I'm not going to do it."

She cocks her head, curious. "Soooo . . . you're going to kill yourself, and your million dollars won't have done you a bit of good. And this is a better outcome than spending the money, saving your life and risking happiness?"

My instinct is to attack, but I can't. She's right. But I still feel like I'm being robbed. "No way three words on a sticky note can change my life."

She gives me that infuriating Mona Lisa smile again and says, "Joe, think back over your life. What's the happiest you've ever been?"

I know the answer in a blink. "The day my daughter Sarah was born. All my troubles fell away as I held that tiny, beautiful baby. I'd heard that every living thing was connected in a cosmic way, but this was the first time I ever knew it was true. It was more than being happy: I felt like I knew what happiness was for the first time ever. I wanted that moment to go on forever."

"Imagine being that happy every day from now on. Would that be worth a million dollars?"

"Yes, absolutely."

She shook my hand and picked up her purse. "You still have twenty-four hours, Joe. I'll see you tomorrow morning at seven."

CHAPTER

6

Back in my room. This is simple: dump the drug into the hooch, swish twice and power it down in a single, decisive gulp. The end. I sit on the bed, working up my nerve, when I hear a voice in my head:

So this is it.

"Yeah, this is it," I say out loud. "I'm really going to do it. Finally."

Okay.

"Okay."

But . . . ummm . . . what if Joan's right?

"C'mon. It's a scam, a rip-off. Three words? No way, no how."

And yet you're curious. You know you are. What have you got to lose?

Oh, man. This is the worst yet. I'm losing an argument to the voice in my head.

The voice says, *So you'll die a day later, so what? That money hasn't bought you a moment's happiness, has it? Buy the note. It's probably a rip-off . . . but if there's a one percent chance it's the bargain of a lifetime. Why not find out?*

What the hell. I pour four fingers of Pappy Van Winkle and cap the bottle. Any more, and I won't have enough for tomorrow. Three words with the power to flip a life from sad to glad . . . could the words be "Pappy Van Winkle"?

Best answer I've come up with so far.

I hope against hope that booze this pricey will ease my journey to the Land of Nod. No such luck. I hear the faintest echo of church bells clanging out "Oh Come All Ye Faithful," and this shakes loose a memory I've been trying to forget for twenty years.

I suddenly remember why I hate Christmas so much.

Sarah was seven. It was 5:00 a.m., Christmas morning. A new bike — the one she had picked out herself, and which I had put together — was next to the tree. I'd worked the day before, and I'd be back on the job tomorrow, but today? Christmas Day? I was looking forward to spending it in my flannel pajamas, peppermint martini in hand, basking in the holiday spirit.

The phone in my home office rang. What the hell? My wife Linda didn't stir. I tiptoed down the hall and picked up.

"Joe, Ted. Get dressed." It was Ted Bickford, Account Executive for my biggest client, a beer that's served in every ballpark and sports arena in the Northern hemisphere. "The car'll be there in twenty minutes, plane leaves in two hours. The old man has an idea for a Super Bowl spot. He's hosting four generations of his family at the compound today, big ol' Christmas party, and he wants you to shoot it and bank the footage. We'll cut it in January. 'From my family to your family, blah blah blah.' I'll meet you at the gate."

Suddenly I was wide awake: face flushed, heart thumping. "It's Christmas day, Ted. My kid, she's been talking about this for a month. I can't just . . ."

"I'm not asking you, Joe, I'm telling you. The old man wants you. C'mon, what's the problem?"

"The problem is . . ." I stopped. I flashed on Ted, recently divorced, no kids. How far was I willing to push this?

"What? Tell me. If you're tired of working on the account, there are plenty of . . ."

"No, no . . ." My mind raced. I was the genius; how could I get out of this? I'd moved heaven and earth to get this account, it was 60 percent of our bookings, and the old man was always pulling stuff like this. He knew he had me. He was a sadist; he lived for this.

"So? We good?"

There it was, the fork in the road. This way, or that? I remember sitting on the edge of my desk, sick to my stomach, staring into space, knowing the right thing to do, what I HAD to do. *Look, Ted, it's Christmas, I'm not going to break my girl's heart. She's seven, I'll never get this day back. Look, we both know it's a simple shoot, I'll get my best guys over there, we'll get hours of sensational B-roll, everything will be fine.*

But I couldn't. I didn't. I choked. I was terrified of losing the account. "Yeah, we're good, Ted. Umm, see you there."

I didn't even have the guts to wake my Linda and Sarah and beg their forgiveness. I got dressed and left a note. "Sorry Sorry Sorry, big work emergency. Love you both! Ho ho ho! Celebrate tomorrow?"

Only there never was a tomorrow. I knew that what I'd done wasn't just one terrible choice: it was a thousand thoughtless choices over the entire span of the marriage. Something died in me knowing that. Actually, several things died. My marriage: Linda couldn't forgive me. My idea of myself as a good, loving father? That died as well. And whatever trust Sarah had in me: gone, gone, gone. Sarah, with those soulful brown eyes. She now knew something about her daddy she'd never forget: that he could be bullied. That supervising a commercial shoot for a third-rate beer was more important than spending Christmas Day with her.

That he loved work more than he loved her.

That's the day I gave up on myself. I stopped trying. Let Linda have Sarah in the divorce. No longer made excuses for missing every school play, every cello recital, her high school and college graduations. Sarah made sure I got an invitation to Linda's funeral after she died from breast cancer, but I didn't go. It took one hell of a lot of bourbon to drown that pain, but I was up to the task. From then on I was dead inside, hung over, going through the motions.

And ever since that day, Christmas has been something to drink my way through. I've never been able to kill the pain, but I can usually deaden it enough to get to January.

CHAPTER 7

December 23

Coffee shop, 7:00 a.m. Joan bustles in, picks up her large holiday peppermint mocha and sits down. "You made it. I'm guessing that means you're ready to buy the note."

"How does this work? It's going to take me some time to . . ."

"Don't worry about the money, we trust you." She pulls her black folio out of the handbag and produces the contract. "This is our standard 'transfer of assets' agreement, including a brief summary of what you've got. You'll have to sell the BMW AND the Apple stock AND the Rolex to get to a million."

I look it over. I'm no longer surprised at what these people know.

Joan asks, "Any questions?"

"If I'm not thrilled I get my money back?"

"Paragraph three, section two. See it?" I nod. "Anything else?"

I feel as if I'm leaving my body. It happened on my wedding day . . . when I saw my baby girl for the first time . . . when I found out my partner was kicking me out of my own business . . . and when I heard my doctor say the words "prostate cancer." A disembodied voice says, "Yeah, I guess we have a deal." The paper gets signed.

"Okay, then." She pulls out a Sharpie and a pad of three inch by five inch yellow-gold sticky notes. She writes three words on the top note, peels it off and hands it to me. I look at it:

GOD

HONESTY

FORGIVENESS

I stare at the words for a long moment.

I feel a rush of mortification—ripped off!—but it fades quickly. I feel like I should tear up the agreement and stalk out, but I don't. Why not? I don't know.

I open my mouth but nothing comes out. Joan puts the folio, the Sharpie and the notes back in her bag, pulls out her smartphone and opens the clock app. "Three days, starting . . . NOW." She shakes my hand. "This is the end, Joe. One way or another, this is it. Fight for your life as hard as we're fighting for it. You're worth it. Good luck."

And with that, Joan walks away.

I feel like an idiot. I start to ball up the sticky note, but stop. Instead I stuff it in my wallet. *Where's the spotlight?* I think, then say aloud, "Ladies and gentlemen, the World's Biggest Sucker!"

No one around me looks up. No one cares. My face is burning as I walk out the door.

CHAPTER

8

I wander the city streets and start to calm down. The rage has vanished, replaced by . . . by what? By curiosity . . . even excitement. There's a kind of grandeur in what I've done. I've either done the dumbest thing in the history of human stupidity (an accomplishment in itself) or . . . *I've saved my life*. Is that even possible? Can a sticky note do that? Can I possibly have done the right thing?

I've got three days. I can stop thinking about this for an hour, right? I'd forgotten the pleasures of people-watching during Christmas, especially young children with their parents. That wide-eyed look of wonder, everything new and radiant: a world aglow. I remember the pure happiness of my daughter, and the joy I felt spending those first six Christmases with her.

When she was five, we got her a handmade, wooden, Barbie-friendly "Magnificent Mansion" dollhouse with five bedrooms and a working elevator. When she came downstairs and saw that thing, she flew into my arms and gave me a boa-constrictor hug that I thought (hoped) would go on forever. As she crushed me, I remembered the feeling I'd had when she was born. I had never really known what love was — real, wholehearted, infinite love — until she came into my life.

My mind pivots back to the note. Of course, it's hopeless. "God, Honesty, Forgiveness." What was George Carlin's line about God? "If there is a God, the best thing you can say about Him is that He has a quality control problem." Amen to that.

Life is a joke, and I'm the punch line.

Honesty? In this life? That's for bank tellers, traffic cops and librarians. Nobody gets anywhere by being honest.

And forgiveness? Am I supposed to forgive my

partner for lying to me, stealing my company and wrecking my career, my life? Am I supposed to forgive my ex for dumping me for doing what I had to do to save the company, and then taking my daughter? Am I supposed to forgive my father for smoking four packs of cigarettes a day, dying of a heart attack when I was nine, leaving me on my own just when I needed him the most? Am I supposed to forgive God for pounding me into the ground like a tent peg?

I think about what Joan said. *No one has ever asked for their money back. Some people have paid a lot more than you. We know a lot about you.*

Who is "we"? Are these the three words that turned everyone else around? I paid a million dollars for these words: everything I own. Where's my "aha!" What am I missing?

And suddenly I'm lower than I've ever been. This one last, crazy hope is vanishing in my rearview mirror. I mean, I'm the guy with the "Life Sucks and then You Die" bumper sticker. The old resolve wells up inside me. It's my life, dammit! I have the perfect right to end it if I want, if there's nothing but pain and misery and despair ahead of me. I chuckle. Was I really dumb enough to think that three words scrawled on a sticky note could change a damn thing? These three words may be the "secret" for some gullible folks, but not for me. Time to end it all.

Then I get a text:

"Want to talk? I've been where you are. Maybe I can help you. Tomorrow? The Ramble? Central Park? 2:00 p.m.?"

I text back a thumbs up. Again, why not? All I need is a miracle.

Just one.

CHAPTER 9

December 24 – Christmas Eve

It's just starting to snow as Joan greets me with a hug. She's snug in a holly-red, cashmere trench coat and a Christmas-tree-green wool beanie cap. She says, "So! Let me guess. You're in despair. The words mean nothing to you, you want your money back, and you're ready to give up and kill yourself. Right?"

I'm so surprised I actually laugh. "You read my mind."

She returns the laugh. "That's where everyone is after the first day. That's why I'm here." We walk over a bridge imagined by Tolkien, through woods from a Robert Frost poem. Winter hush, a silent snowfall drifting down and coating the landscape in perfect white. I feel like we're in a snow globe held by a child in a Hallmark Christmas movie.

"Tell me what I'm missing."

"Okay, says Joan. She looks up at the dancing snowflakes and catches one on the end of her tongue. Still looking up, she says, "Let's start with God."

"There is no God."

She turns to me. "I'm not talking about the grumpy guy in the Old Testament hurling thunderbolts from His heavenly perch, Joe. I'm talking about Einstein's question."

"Einstein's question?"

"Albert Einstein said the most important question we can ask is, 'Is the Universe friendly?' If we decide it's not, we'll be driven by fear and spend our lives fighting phantoms and building higher walls and better weapons to destroy our so-called enemies."

"Sounds about right," I say.

Joan smiles. "Do you know the story of Job? From the Bible?"

That seems like a pretty abrupt left turn, but . . . "Not really. I know that . . . let's see . . . Satan makes a bet with God that Satan can turn God's most righteous disciple against him if God tortures him enough. Job ends up in a hair shirt, covered with boils, screaming at God. Is that right?"

"Except for the most important part."

"Which is?

"God takes everything from Job—his worldly possessions, his family, and finally his health. Job finally snaps. He shakes his fist at God and says, 'Why are you doing this to me? Don't you have a plan for me?' And do you know what God says? This is the last time God ever speaks to Man in the Bible."

"No. What does he say?"

Joan stops, takes my hand, and looks me right in the eye. "God says, 'Yes, I have a plan for you. But it's not for you to know what it is.'"

Time stops. The world around me is

tomb-silent as the words echo in my mind. "It's not for me . . ."

" . . . to know what it is. That's right, Joe. Don't you see? You've been living your life like we all do, like I did until I came to this moment in my own journey."

As if I'd conjured it from a dream, a hot chocolate kiosk appears next to a frozen pond where bundled-up parents skate with their squealing young ones. I buy one for each of us and savor the burn of that scalding cocoa quenched with cool whipped cream and marshmallows: I'm having a virgin Irish coffee, without the coffee!

We sip and stroll. I'm fixed on Joan's every word. I'm not just listening, I'm feeling what she says deep inside myself. Something's happening. What is it? She says, "We live our lives like Job did, as if we've got a deal with God. We make up a story about what pleasing God looks like, and then we assume that if we follow the rules, nothing bad will ever happen to us. We won't get dumped, or divorced, or fired or get cancer." She stops again, looks at me. "But the thing is, Joe, we don't have a deal with God. Never have, never did. There are no rules, just the ones we make up ourselves. God's plan for us is a secret. And that makes all the difference."

I drop my cup in a trashcan and stare up at that beautiful snowy sky. I know she's right. And if she's right, that changes everything. All I can think to ask is, "Why?"

"You're angry because at some level you feel God is punishing you for breaking rules that never existed. What if..."

"Yes? What if what?" I'm laser-focused, like I've waited my whole life for the answer to this question.

She doffs the beanie and shakes off some frost. "What if God's secret plan for you — the one you'll never, ever know until you're at those pearly gates — is for you to have this very crisis . . . which leads you to crash into little ol' me . . . so I can make you this ridiculous deal . . . so the two of us can take this lovely walk in this beautiful park? And on this walk, as we sip our hot chocolate and dance between the snowflakes, I make these three beautiful words come alive for you in a way that awakens something that's always been inside you, that's been sleeping since the day you were born . . . and in so doing, help you save your precious life?"

"What's been sleeping inside me?"

Joan smiles. "The truth, Joe. Are you ready for the truth?"

Am I? My heart is thudding in my chest. "I . . . I think so."

"The truth is that you've been living in a friendly universe all along, with air to breathe and water to drink and Mozart to listen to and ice cream to eat and roses to smell and people to love . . . And you've been so locked into your grim, self-invented nightmare world that you've missed all of it."

I try to fight this, but I'm not just hearing her words—they're bypassing my brain, going straight to my soul. "So if I've been lying to myself about the very nature of God and the universe . . ."

"You've been trapped in a world of fear, using anger as a shield against your demons. That's why the second word is "honesty." Honesty means letting go of all those soul-destroying lies you thought you needed to survive. Time to get honest, Joe. See life for what it is, and yourself for who you are. Who are you, Joe?"

"A failure," I say. "A loser. An alcoholic. Unsuccessful, unloved, unwanted. Garbage."

"Okay. And what's underneath all those judgments?"

"Underneath?"

"Honesty, Joe. Be honest. Are you . . . creative?"

"Well, I've got seven bookshelves of advertising awards."

"So the answer is yes. Picasso once said the greatest artist of all is God, because God will try anything. Like a platypus, or the squidworm, or the corpse flower. And you, my friend, are an open channel of this cosmic creativity. You've got the hardware to prove it."

"Yeah, I guess."

"Creative. And you told me you fell in love with your daughter when she was born. So you're filled with love."

"Not at the moment."

"But that love is inside you: the love that binds the universe. The love you felt on that Christmas morning. It's in all of us, Joe. It just needs to be awakened."

"I guess . . ."

"And inspirational? Any of your colleagues go on to better things because of you?"

"Sure."

"How about wise? Humble? Compassionate?"

I snort. "Definitely not. Smart maybe, but wise? I don't . . ."

She steps in front of me. Stops me cold. Grabs me by the shoulders. "Shall we see if you just might be those three things, right here, right now?"

CHAPTER

10

"**O**-okay." I don't know where this is going, but then I haven't known where anything's been going for a week now. And I feel like I'm moving toward something: something vital.

"Forgiveness, Joe. This is the big one. The final exam."

"Yeah, right. So I'm supposed to forgive everybody for betraying me, hurting me, screwing me over. I'm supposed to forgive . . ."

"That's not why this word is on the sticky note."

"Then why . . ."

"This is about forgiving yourself, Joe."

"Forgiving . . . forgiving myself?"

"Forgiving yourself for shadow-boxing in your nightmare world of anger and fear, pushing people away, reaching for something to make yourself feel better—another account, another woman, another drink, another award. But it never worked, did it? Not for long, anyway. And meanwhile you've been missing your chance, Joe. Missing your chance to stroll through Mr. Einstein's friendly universe."

"That makes me stupid, not wise."

"You're wise because you can feel—not with your head, but your heart—that I'm right about you. And humble, because you've been so wrong for so long that you're willing to let it all go, start anew, and try a new way of looking at life. And compassionate because you love yourself enough to give me every dollar you've got in this world for the chance of saving yourself. And what that million dollars buys you is the chance to forgive yourself. Forgive yourself for making everything about *you*, Joe. What you want, and your anger at not getting it. Forgive yourself for living so much of your life ignoring the mystery, the wonder, the beauty, and, yes, the terror of being alive. Can you forgive yourself for becoming so consumed by your own nightmare of rage and disappointment that you missed the real adventure? The life you were put here to live?"

I can feel hot tears running down my cheeks. "And now that life is gone . . ."

"NO, Joe! It's not! Can't you see it? The chance I'm offering you is the biggest, best chance you'll ever have. It's a chance that's always been there, not just for you but for every one of us. It's a chance that was given to me, and since I took it, it's been at the center of my life. Imagine a life, Joe, where every moment is an act of love, generosity and kindness. Where you get to do for other suffering souls what I'm doing for you, right here, right now. Where every single morning is a fresh, new, beautiful opportunity to give yourself away to others, to serve them and to love them with the joy you had on that morning so long ago holding your beautiful daughter. The chance to become God's holy fool, joining a fellowship of like-minded fools who have come together for no other reason than to savor the paradoxical rapture of getting a million dollars' worth of pleasure by giving ourselves away in service."

"You mean . . . you mean join you in . . . in whatever this is you do?"

"Well," she said, "you're broke and you need a job. Why not?"

I'm in shock. Is this a dream, and I'll wake up in my old life? Or is this what's real, and I've just awakened from a lifetime-long nightmare into some new realm of bliss?

Is this ecstasy, or delirium?

Joan says, "You've still got twenty-four hours, Joe. Use them all. If you want your old life back, just let me know. But if you want more of what you're feeling right now —" she smiles at me, one friend to another " — that feeling of love you're pushing down with all your might, that feeling that you're ready to connect with the love that binds this friendly universe together — you can have that as well. Trust what's in your heart, Joe. Enjoy the rest of this beautiful, perfect day, and call me tomorrow."

CHAPTER

11

I watch her vanish, and then . . . what's this? I've got that "third drink" feeling: giddy, weightless and carefree, but I'm clear-headed and cold sober. There's no pain in my body, just a surprised rush of gladness, shocked at the pure pleasure of being alive in this moment.

As I wander out of Central Park into the city, I revel in a delicious clash of paradoxical feelings. I'm joyous that I've saved my own life (with a little help). Suddenly I feel *necessary* to the universe, that there are people I have to meet to share what I know, so they can feel like I do. I'm ambitious! I'm eager! And at the same time I feel a bit of melancholy that I've squandered so many years marinating in despair and self-pity. I want to hug every single person I meet, and I'm content to ramble along by my lonesome. I'm amazed at this outlandish intervention by this improbable cabal of good-doers, and satisfied that my life couldn't possibly have turned out any other way.

I'm in a kind of ecstatic fog. I haven't just "learned" something: I've acquired a new filter for being in the world. No, that's not quite right. The old, stale "fear" filter I'd used to experience the world has vaporized, and now there's no filter at all. I'm seeing this beautiful, friendly world—really SEEING it—for the first time.

I find myself on Broadway, in front of Zabar's. I've passed this place a million times, never given it a second thought. Now I wander into this dazzling dreamland and gaze at the happy, chattering Christmas Eve crowd. I'm dumbstruck by the bustling theater of the place: all these lovely folks gathered in a cathedral of gastronomic bliss. An emporium designed to satiate every hunger, quench every thirst, fill every sense, gratify every desire! Just the simplest thing—a toasted bagel, a schmear of cream cheese, some slices of lox topped with red onions and capers, washed down with a scalding cup of dark roast coffee—makes me weep.

Einstein! Can you hear me? It's me, Joe Dolan, answering your question! Friendly universe, yes! Here's proof!

I might have missed this if I'd murdered myself.

But no, I'm alive. And it's a miracle.

God. Honesty. Forgiveness. Three words. I've heard them individually a million times, but never in this specific cascade, and I've never really understood them until now. I let them tumble through my mind as I amble through Manhattan back to my hotel. Now I'm eating hot, sugar-roasted pecans out of a paper cone as I see a delighted four-year-old girl grapple with a giant stuffed T-Rex as her father holds its neck. I hear music, a celestial harmonic Passion. It's coming from a church, up ahead. I walk inside a majestic Gothic revival chamber and plop down in the back row. Christmas Eve service.

Another small miracle: they're singing the "Agnus Dei," the vocal version of Samuel Barber's ethereal *Adagio for Strings*. Weeping! Not again! Yes again, for the sheer improbable wonder of it all! There's this thing we humans have pulled from the heavens, called "music"! And we've evolved it over thousands of years into this exquisite expression of pure emotion, channeled by Barber from some celestial realm into notes on a page to be sung by this conspiracy of angels in this resonant brownstone sanctuary in this infinite moment for the elevation of my spirit and soul.

When the Minister takes the pulpit, I flee. What words can possibly compete with that music? I'm wrung out, ready for sleep. One more day . . . and I know what my answer is going to be.

CHAPTER

12

Christmas Day

U p at first light. I'm alive! Thank you Great Unknowable Oneness for saving me from myself. I am Ebenezer Scrooge: light as a feather, happy as an angel, merry as a schoolboy, giddy as a drunken man! I am George Bailey, running down the main street of Bedford Falls yelling, "I'm going to jail! Isn't it wonderful!" I hum "Joy to the World" as I flush a thousand dollars of Chinese toxicants down the toilet, chased with a bottle of twenty-three-year-old 95.6 proof Kentucky Straight Bourbon Whiskey.

What to do? Where to go? I know! I'm off to the HuggaMug for an experiment. I order a large dark roast and hand the barista a $100 bill. "Free coffee for the next twenty people, and don't tell anyone who is buying." I take a seat and watch as customer after customer lights up. Each customer insists on donating a cup to the next one in line, and five hours later not a single person has paid for their own coffee. Better yet, people are talking to one another trying to figure out how this all started. Hugs, laughter, toasts, and the gifts! Mugs, hats, tumblers, aprons, and bags of beans change hands. I slip out, aglow.

Back in the hotel to make two phone calls. The first is the easy one. I call Joan Blair. Yes, I'm in. Thank you from the bottom of my overflowing heart. Best Christmas ever.

Then the hard one. I call my daughter. My hands are trembling: I have to punch in the numbers three times to get it right.

"Hello, Sarah? It's Joe. Your father." She's shocked, and almost hangs up. I practically scream "I LOVE YOU."

Silence.

Then I just begin talking. I have the word "HONESTY" in front of me on the hotel notepad in big block letters. I begin with another Christmas morning, when she was seven years old and I did something unforgivable, which I made much worse by wallowing in my disgrace, spiraling down a rathole of self-hate and taking it as a given that she would never forgive me. I speak for forty minutes and end by saying, "And I don't expect you to forgive me now, but I can't go on without you knowing that I love you more than life itself. I always have, always will. You are a dream I dreamed that came true, a once-only-in-the-history-of-the-universe miracle, a perfect expression of God's loving grace."

And with that I stop speaking.

More silence. Thirty seconds, a minute, two minutes. Is she still there?

Then sniffling, and then, "Oh, Daddy." The sweetest words I'll ever hear. We talk for another two hours. Then I talk to my grandkids, Abigail and Noah for another hour.

We make arrangements, and I fly to Chicago the next day.

It's a magnificent reunion. We laugh about the money. She never counted on it. She assumed I'd blow it in Las Vegas or have it cremated along with me when I died. We have a perfect, perfectly ordinary time catching up and singing carols and watching cartoons and feasting on roast turkey and, most of all, laughing, crying and hugging.

And the entire time, I think to myself, *God bless us every one: even me.*

CHAPTER

13

December 24, Christmas Eve, One Year Later

I hope that you never find yourself in a situation as dire as the one I was in. If you do, I pray you wander into my bar before you do anything rash. I'll make you the best damn Irish coffee you ever tasted, and I'll make sure it gets placed on top of just the right napkin.

All you have to do is call the number. That's it! And buy the sticky note, have the meeting, and do the hard work of forgiving yourself, because there's nothing like the joy of waking up in Einstein's friendly universe for another day filled with the wonders of forgiveness, compassion, honesty and unconditional love. I've been living in that universe for a year now and it just gets better every day.

This evening I'll celebrate Christmas with Sarah and Abigail and Noah. And as I gaze on that glorious scene, I'll think to myself,

A million for a sticky note? Best money I ever spent.

EPILOGUE

Why This, Why Now?

There's a Hindu parable that goes something like this:

The gods are bickering over where to hide the secret of life so that mortals will never find it. "Bury it under a mountain, they'll never find it there."

"No," says another, "They'll dig it up. Hide it in the depths of the deepest ocean, it will be safe there."

"They are clever, these people. Someday they'll invent the means to explore the oceans." They all nod. Where then?

Finally, another god says, "Put it inside them.

They'll never think of looking for it there." They agree. And so the secret of life was hidden within us. We carry it with us as we go through our days searching "out there" for it. And the gods laugh and shake their heads.

You're probably wondering why I'm revealing the secret that cost me a million dollars—and others a lot more—for the price of an everyday book. I'm doing it because this is a secret that is meant to be shared. It's hiding in plain sight. It's inside you, as it was inside me. The Service didn't come together to make money. It is now and has always been a covert confederacy of saved souls dedicated to hoodwinking the despondent into remaking themselves as joyous vessels of peace, gladness and compassion.

I've cleared it with Joan, of course. She'd be delighted if the Service ran out of customers. She figures we'll still get folks who will never see this book, who will miss the message, and who will need the Service. And we'll be there for them.

I'm still astonished this happened to me: that God really does have a plan for me, and a part of that plan involved me plummeting down an elevator shaft of despair so I could land on a bed of marshmallows in the Garden of Grace and Redemption. That I'd be saved by a group that invited me to impoverish myself for a three-word sticky note thrills me to the marrow of my bones and makes me howl with laughter even today.

And the idea that I can share this secret with you? That fills me with happiness.

Let me tell you how I use the secret in my everyday life: and I do use it, every single day.

Every morning I wake up and think, "I've got a million dollars in my pocket." This money just happens to be in the form of the sticky note that I had laminated two weeks after I bought it. I run into the same number of troubles and travails that you do in your everyday life. The difference is that I have the note to bring me back to my purpose, which is to forget myself by helping others experience the life-changing epiphany I enjoyed. And since you can only keep what you give away, I get to enjoy my own epiphany every time I help someone have theirs.

Because of the note, I ask myself an entirely

different set of questions when I encounter a challenge. An example is my diagnosis of prostate cancer. When I heard the words "You've got cancer" come out of that doctor's mouth, my monkey-mind went berserk. Every nightmare I'd ever had was about to come true. I was about to suffer a lonely, agonizing death. It's one of the reasons I'd decided to hurry things up with that pharmaceutical knock-out punch.

Now I stare at the first word of the note — GOD — and ask myself this question:

What's the cosmic gift in this diagnosis? After all, I'm living in Einstein's friendly universe, so there must be a gift. And I quickly realize that hearing those words has made me understand how precious every single moment of life is. All I've got is this one beautiful perfect day. Why waste a moment on brooding and negativity? I can get high on LSD: Laughing, Singing and Dancing. I can spend this moment listening to a favorite piece of music, connecting with my daughter, watching children frolic on a playground, taking a walk in a botanical garden, or doing the work of helping others (the most fun you can have with your clothes on).

I keep a quotes diary, and one of my favorites is from the writer John Updike: "America is a vast conspiracy to make you happy." If I really need a pick-me-up, I walk through any commercial district in my hometown. This is all here to make me happy! Me, personally! Look, there's the coffee place where my life changed. Coffee, what a miracle! That shop sells a beverage that defies the laws of thermodynamics. It buoys the spirit and delivers a joyous jolt of energy to the brain and yet it has absolutely no food value! No calories, fats, carbohydrates or protein. And I can walk right in and buy sixteen ounces of joy every single morning.

And there's the place that sold me my smartphone, which is also my watch, my portable music player, my email and messaging device, my news aggregator, my podcast player, my device for playing recorded books and my personal health monitor. Again (I say this a lot), what a miracle! And there's a department store that has gathered thousands of items from around the world just in case I decide that something in there might make my life better. And a bookstore! A million stories to enjoy, get lost in, or—more importantly—"get found in." And a street vendor selling bagels and candied cashews! Everywhere I turn, I see people who show up every day just to make me happy. How cool is that?

Now I look at the second word—HONESTY. Here I might ask myself this question:

"If you take away all your history and all your fear and all your made-up premonitions of doom, what's actually going on with you, right this second?" I take a very deep breath, and I remember how lucky I am. There are two kinds of prostate cancer, and I've got the "good" kind. That is, my kind grows very slowly, and only requires a strategy of "watchful waiting" to make sure it doesn't turn into the bad, aggressive, life-threatening kind. The biggest blessing of the cancer is this: it's caused me to give up all my vices and adopt a health regimen, including exercise and a healthy diet, that is very likely to add twenty pleasurable years to my life. I only have one Irish coffee a year now, on Christmas Day with my daughter. I'm almost certain to die of something else before I die of this.

And then I remember that day in Central Park and the word HONESTY expands to embrace my entire outlook for being in the world. If I'm honest with myself, I realize that almost everyone I meet in an average day is deeply inclined to be good to me, and to one another. The honest approach to life is to be courageous: do as much good for as many people as possible. Be generous. Share something with everyone: a smile, a joke, a helping hand, or a cup of coffee (I still buy coffee for people). I'm no longer hypnotized by the news, which only reports the very worst about humanity (because that's what's unusual!) I look around and I see what should be on the front page: parents hugging their kids, airliners landing safely, drivers stopping at red lights, hopeful young people falling in love, and folks working together out of compassion to make the world a better place.

I'm feeling pretty good by now. I don't really need to continue, but of course the third word— FORGIVENESS—is maybe the most important of the three. I know that if I can forgive myself for what I've done in the past, I can create the life I want in the future. When I struggle to forgive myself, I ask these questions:

- When I made that mistake, was I doing the best I could with what I knew at the time?

- Did I learn from what happened?

- If my best friend did what I did, would I forgive her?

The answers are always Yes, Yes, and Of course.

The Indian poet Rabindranath Tagore wrote this:

"Let me not pray to be sheltered from dangers but to be fearless in facing them. Let me not beg for the stilling of my pain but for the heart to conquer it. Let me not crave in anxious fear to be saved but hope for the patience to win my freedom."

The Sticky Note tells me that I'm the hero of my own blessed adventure. In this friendly universe I can be fearless in facing whatever danger presents itself. I no longer need to numb myself from my pain; instead, I can face it and heal the wound causing it. And I can become a peaceful warrior, winning my freedom by fighting for the freedom of others.

The Importance of Stories

Since this blessed note came into my life, I look at movies and TV shows in a whole different way. I have a kind of X-ray vision into stories I never had before. And what I notice is that there's a single story—based on the story of Job that Joan shared with me—that we humans can't stop telling ourselves. It's almost as if—in fact, it's EXACTLY as if—we have created this thing called "narrative storytelling" as a magical process that bypasses the conscious mind and reaches into what Jung called the "collective unconscious" to wake us all up. Wake us up to what? To the idea that we got ourselves into whatever mess we're wallowing in for the very purpose of finding compassion for ourselves, forgiving ourselves, and then extending that compassion to all of humanity.

Want an example? Is there a more popular, oft-told story in the world than *A Christmas Carol* by Charles Dickens? This is the story of a selfish, bitter man—a man with no virtues—who is offered the astonishing (and terrifying) chance to view his past, present and future. In so doing, he sees how—like me—he was living in a hell of his own making. He literally wakes up to a new life of kindness, love and generosity. This story speaks to millions of people around the world. Why? Because we've all got a little (or, in my case, a lot) of Scrooge in us. When Scrooge begs the Ghost of Christmas Yet-to-Come for another chance, he's begging for forgiveness. And then Dickens wipes the slate clean, and Scrooge gets a second chance at life.

Just like I got. And like Scrooge, I'm not wasting it.

I'm using it to share what I've learned with you.

The End

Acknowledgments

I'd like to acknowledge Maurice Bassett, who took a chance on me, and Chris Nelson, who did such a great job shaping the manuscript and correcting all my errors. I'd like to acknowledge the courageous writers (see dedication) who battle this corrosive culture and offer practical solutions for positive change. And finally I'd like to acknowledge that long-forgotten reporter on NPR who, thirty years ago, did a feature story on a survey of psychologists and reported that each of them had come to rely on a certain three words to heal people. Thank goodness I pulled over and wrote those words down.

About the Author

The author, R. Lee Procter, is a writer living in the Los Angeles area. He has worked in advertising, television and location-based entertainment (theme parks, museums, etc.). He was a Groundling alongside Pee Wee Herman and Phil Hartman and an Imagineer for the Walt Disney Company. Like most people, he's interested in making the world a better, happier place.

You can contact R. Lee Procter at:

milliondollarstickynote@gmail.com

A full-color, coffee-table style photo album of 67 previously unpublished and seldom-seen photos of Jackie Kennedy from her childhood and teen years.

There must be hundreds of thousands of photos of Jackie Kennedy (1929-1994), our much-loved First Lady, either with or without President John F. Kennedy, but what you are about to experience in *Early Jackie* is strikingly different from the well-known and classic Jackie photos. These are the "lost" photos of Jackie from when she was known—prior to marriage—by the name of "Jackie Bouvier."

Jackie Kennedy lovers everywhere will delight in owning this remarkable, full-color photo album!

MAURICE BASSETT

Publisher's Catalogue

The Mahatma Gandhi Library

#1 Towards Non-Violent Politics

* * *

The Prosperous Series

#1 The Prosperous Coach: Increase Income and Impact for You and Your Clients (Steve Chandler and Rich Litvin)

#2 The Prosperous Hip Hop Producer: My Beat-Making Journey from My Grandma's Patio to a Six-Figure Business (Curtiss King)

#3 The Prosperous Hotelier (David Lund)

* * *

Devon Bandison

Fatherhood Is Leadership: Your Playbook for Success, Self-Leadership, and a Richer Life

Roy G. Biv

1921: A Celebration of Toned 1921 Peace Dollars as Numismatic Art

Dancing on Antique Toning: A Further Celebration of Numismatic Art

Dancing on Rainbows: A Celebration of Numismatic Art

Early Jackie: The "Lost" Photos of Jackie Bouvier

Sir Fairfax L. Cartwright

The Mystic Rose from the Garden of the King

Steve Chandler

37 Ways to BOOST Your Coaching Practice: PLUS: the 17 Lies That Hold Coaches Back and the Truth That Sets Them Free

50 Ways to Create Great Relationships

Business Coaching (Steve Chandler and Sam Beckford)

Crazy Good: A Book of CHOICES

CREATOR

Death Wish: The Path through Addiction to a Glorious Life

Fearless: Creating the Courage to Change the Things You Can

How to Get Clients: New Pathways to Coaching Prosperity

The Prosperous Coach: Increase Income and Impact for You and Your Clients (The Prosperous Series #1) (Steve Chandler and Rich Litvin)

RIGHT NOW: Mastering the Beauty of the Present Moment

Shift Your Mind Shift The World (Revised Edition)

Time Warrior: How to defeat procrastination, people-pleasing, self-doubt, over-commitment, broken promises and chaos

Wealth Warrior: The Personal Prosperity Revolution

Curtiss King

The Prosperous Hip Hop Producer: My Beat-Making Journey from My Grandma's Patio to a Six-Figure Business (The Prosperous Series #2)

David Lindsay

A Blade for Sale: The Adventures of Monsieur de Mailly

Rich Litvin

The Prosperous Coach: Increase Income and Impact for You and Your Clients (The Prosperous Series #1) (Steve Chandler and Rich Litvin)

David Lund

The Prosperous Hotelier (The Prosperous Series #3)

John G. W. Mahanna

The Human Touch: My Friendship and Work with President John F. Kennedy

Abraham H. Maslow

The Aims of Education (audio)

The B-language Workshop (audio)

Being Abraham Maslow (DVD)

The Eupsychian Ethic (audio)

The Farther Reaches of Human Nature (audio)

Maslow and Self-Actualization (DVD)

Maslow on Management (audiobook)

Personality and Growth: A Humanistic Psychologist in the

Classroom

Psychology and Religious Awareness (audio)

The Psychology of Science: A Reconnaissance

Self-Actualization (audio)

Weekend with Maslow (audio)

R. Lee Procter

The Million-Dollar Sticky Note: 3 Words that Can Change Your Life

Harold E. Robles

Albert Schweitzer: An Adventurer for Humanity

Albert Schweitzer

Reverence for Life: The Words of Albert Schweitzer

Patrick O. Smith

ACDF: The Informed Patient: My journey undergoing neck fusion surgery

William Tillier

Abraham H. Maslow: A Comprehensive Bibliography

Personality Development through Positive Disintegration: The Work of Kazimierz Dąbrowski

Margery Williams

The Velveteen Rabbit: or How Toys Become Real